The Secret Ways of Prayer

VOLUME THREE

The Carmel Series on Christian Life
Under the Direction of
Father Kieran Kavanaugh, O.C.D.

The Secret Ways of Prayer

by

R. L. Bruckberger, O. P.

DIMENSION BOOKS

WILKES-BARRE, PA.

Published by Dimension Books
Wilkes-Barre, Pa.

This is a translation of *Rejoindre Dieu* by R. L. Bruckberger, O.P. (Paris: Gallimard) This English version has been made from the French edition by Salvator Attanasio.

Library of Congress Catalog Card Number 64-19474

Nihil Obstat
Rev. James F. Smurl, S.T.D.
Censor Librorum
April 15th, 1964

Imprimatur
✠ Jerome D. Hannon
Bishop of Scranton
April 17th, 1964

Contents

Foreword

There are four different sections in this little book, but they actually form just varying aspects of a single theme. I chose the arrangement they here possess to try to emphasize one distinctive, even unique privilege of Christian devotion—namely, how it can bring about union with God through strictly material things like the Humanity of Christ and the Christian Sacraments.

There is a development of this theme from one chapter to another. Everything, for example, that is said about prayer at the beginning of the book can be effectively applied later on in the chapter dealing with our devotion to the Eucharistic Presence of Christ.

The book is certainly, obviously, not exhaustive. My aim has rather been to suggest certain primordial elements of Christianity and to draw out of them the fundamentals of Christian piety and prayer.

"I have cried to the Lord with my voice . . . O Lord, thou wilt open my lips: and my mouth shall declare thy praise." (Ps. 3:5)

Seek and You Shall Find

CHRISTIANITY, alone among many religions, has revealed to the world the possibilities of loving intimacy with God. From its beginnings, it has spoken of the life of God within us as well as the supernatural qualities that belong to divine love. This love, it has always emphasized, is expressed by us in two great gifts of our selfhood—love of our neighbor and prayer. These are two essentially *Christian* ways of loving God, so much so that we Christians can recognize whether the love inspiring us comes from God by the signs which dispose us to a deep affection for our neighbor and for the life of prayer.

These two things spring from one source, love

of God; and the first and indeed only commandment Christ has left to us, and one whose observance may obtain for us his friendship, will always be this: "Thou shalt love the Lord thy God with thy whole heart, and with thy whole soul, and with thy whole mind, and with thy whole strength."

What is new here is not the formula itself. That already existed in the ancient law of the Hebrews. Before Christ, however, it was never considered sufficient unto itself; sufficient for guaranteeing the very substance of religion. Jesus asserted that the content of this commandment embodied all the acts of true religion, embraced all the obligations of the true servant of God. In contrast, a life full of outwardly devotional practices but lacking in this love of God (and in its two-fold realization in prayer and love of neighbor) would be a phantom Christian life. It would be a life without supernatural meaning. It would be an illusion.

There is hardly a single Christian who at some time or other in his life has not desired to love God with all his heart; aspired to a perfect union of such quality that he would no longer be able to tear himself away from God again. "Be no longer a stranger unto me, O Lord!" How many there are who have repeatedly and faithfully sought this lofty love, prayed God for it in all sincerity, boldly and trustingly implored it of His Sacred Heart. It not infrequently happens, however, that we feel God is inattentive to such prayer, indeed that he is rejecting us.

Yet it is impossible for God to deceive us. We can be assured by what is written in the Gospel: "What man is there among you who, if his son asks him for a loaf, will hand him a stone; or if he asks for a fish, will hand him a serpent? If therefore you (evil as you are) know how to give good gifts to your children, how much more will your Father in heaven give good things to those who ask Him for them!" Such a solemn promise is unbreakable. It would be blasphemous to believe that God has not at least as much compassion as we human beings, and there is no one of us so hard-hearted as to give a serpent to his hungry child who asks him for something to eat. Similarly, no matter how morally wretched a man might be, God cannot but allow him to love Him, if he appeals to this promise and to his rightful claim as a child of God. God can never go back on His given word, for His very essence is love and fidelity.

Hence the fundamental spirit of Christian prayer must always be to put God face to face with His promise, to say to Him once and for all: "I am your exceedingly wretched child, but nevertheless *yours.* I ask you for your love which is more necessary to me than daily bread, and I shall never give up until you grant it to me."

Many Christians have spoken these words at one time or another in their lives. Many have begun to pray with all the strength of their wills, vehemently, heroically, constantly. They have set out on a search for the face of God, and they have done so with great generosity because their lives seem lusterless and cold without Him, useless, not worth the effort of living them. They are not naive people. It seemed to them that God alone mattered, and that if they could only encounter God face to face (be it even in the night), if they could only meet Him just once, their lackluster lives would be quickened and divinized by the encounter, would be thoroughly transfigured from one end to the other. For a religious person, what could be more logical than such an attitude. An electric cable has a very high potential; we would be instantly felled as though by lightning were we merely to touch it. Yet God is a Being with a much greater energy-charge than lightning or electricity. He is a living Being, reactive and explosive, so full of life that merely to touch Him for an instant would suffice to melt our souls with love as if they had been plunged into a fiery furnace. Is it possible to believe that contact with God could do otherwise than renew our lives and transfigure our souls?

The answer to this question is obvious, but it not infrequently proves to be the wrong question for us to ask. Actually, despite long and sustained effort on the part of generous and sincere souls, no contact with God is achieved. The soul believes itself to be swamped in the same supernatural lethargy as troubled it before it began its search. When it compares its efforts with the mediocre quality of the love it experiences, it feels that it has been duped, that God has not kept His promise. Under the weight of disappointment the soul falls back on itself, turns away from God, believing that God has not yet willed to yield to its importunities.

The truth is that an essential factor for confrontation with God is frequently missing from our prayers. We know that the slightest amount of insulation is enough to prevent electrical contact between two wires. Similarly, though a man or woman may strive mightily to draw nearer to God, there may always remain an obstacle between them and the Master. It may be only the slightest thing—something hardly perceptible to our consciousness. Nevertheless, it is this which keeps the soul isolated from God, insulated from Him. It is as if one built an enormous electrical plant to satisfy his needs, but didn't bother to connect the wall-plugs whose function is to deliver the energy and spark everything, lighting up all the lamps and heating all the radiators.

How many lives, outwardly so fine and Christian, are really like these lavishly equipped and complex installations, where God's current of love never flows or does so only with a derisive trickle. It is better to have just one small lamp provided it be really lit, so that our souls may remain in touch with the source of light, than to deceive ourselves with illusions and chimeras, none of which profit anything. Let us examine this idea of contact more closely, the nature of its requirements and the conditions under which it may be achieved.

My chemistry teacher in college was a very

sensible man and what he told us always seemed to be of a quite practical nature. He always tried to demonstrate exactly what he was saying. At the introduction to any of his experiments, he would say: "Let us put two bodies together; for example, this sulphuric acid and this copper." This sort of thing, I understand, is a ritual formula among chemists, and serves as a prelude to all their experiments. It is not without its lesson for the spiritual life. Most of the prayers we say invariably begin with an analogous formula: "Let us put ourselves in the presence of God."

These two expressions have similar meanings, and we should try to understand the second by the first. My chemistry teacher always joined the gesture with the word. When he said "Let us put sulphuric acid and copper together," he would actually take a portion of each from their respective containers and proceed to mix them before our eyes. But when a Christian says: "Let us put ourselves in the presence of God," does he ever do anything with God, is it possible for him to do anything with Him? Actually, he leaves God right where He is, and most often does the same with himself. He makes no effort to effect a severance from selfhood in order to try to unite himself to God. Under these conditions we may be sure that nothing at all will happen, that no "reaction" of God will take place in the soul. Thus, the first and essential requirement of prayer is *that of putting ourselves in the presence of God*. But to do this, we must understand who God is and what way we might be able to unite ourselves to Him.

However banal it might appear, we can never insist too much that God is not a creature but the Creator of all things. He is outside, completely and entirely outside, the circle of creation. We might roam through the whole universe and search every corner of it; we would never come face to face with God, find Him as He is in Himself. He is infinitely above everything we see and hear and observe in the world. We can neither overtake Him, nor fathom Him, nor embrace Him as we do a creature. In order to encounter Him, we must transcend everything, we must go beyond all. As long as we are preoccupied with creatures, no matter who or what, it is not God who is at the center of our attention. Let us take the word "occupy" in its most concrete meaning. When we say that God must occupy our attention, we should keep in mind such expressions as "occupy a territory or house," or "occupy a tent." Actually the ideal requirement of prayer is suggested more properly in this latter expression where God would occupy us as a camper does his tent, and contact with Him would be at its maximum and from all sides. Nothing less would be achieved than a total habitation of ourselves by God.

If, then, I allow myself to be concerned with creatures when I am praying, they are more within me than God is. I am in contact with them and not with God; since God is not one of them, He remains absent from me. He is not with me as He is in Himself; He does not occupy the center of my attention. He can of course be with me through His grace, but it is as if He met me in someone else's house rather than in my own. He has competition for the middle of the stage, and no intimacy is possible under these conditions. He is like us in this respect; and as much as He loves us, He would not choose a place full of people to divulge His secrets to us.

Putting ourselves in God's presence, which is the preliminary step to all prayer, is very similar (though reversely) to temptation. In temptation, it is a matter of knowing whether we will cut ourselves off from God and attach ourselves by preference to a creature. In prayer, it is a matter of knowing whether (and how) we can attach ourselves to God alone, in Himself. The basic requirement for achieving this latter attachment is to cut ourselves off, at least momentarily, from everything that is not God.

It is quite possible for us to be attached to several creatures at the same time. They are not always incompatible with each other; in fact they mutually complement each other in most of our affairs in life and business. But when we want to unite ourselves to God as He is in Himself, things are different. Then we must remember that God is perfectly self-sufficient, and the search for Him is totally incompatible with love of anything not identifiable with Him. Since He is all perfect, He must take the place of everything else.

When we want to put ourselves in His presence, the first thing to do is to recognize His excellence, to accept it as a matter of fact in an act of total and absolute reverence by complete indifference to all creatures. It is as if we are preparing the streets for a great King to pass through them. At the moment the King is to pass by, no matter how the streets are otherwise used and by how many people, the road is cleared exclusively for him. Thus when we begin to pray, let us clear a broad passageway in our souls and keep all creatures behind what we might call an honorary reviewing line. The most basic necessity of all is to pay homage to God. He is our Sovereign—and so jealous a Ruler that if we are attending to many other matters and persons, we will miss Him. He would become just another face in the crowd.

Prayer's fundamental effort, then, is similar to the one we make to resist temptation. In temptation our sensibility, our imagination and sometimes the lower regions of our will are all powerfully drawn towards an object that would cut us off from God, were we to acquiesce in an attachment to it. But at its summit, our will maintains an unsullied and devoted attachment to God, no matter what the cost. All the soul's fidelity finds refuge in this pinnacle of the spirit and wholly expresses itself by an almost desperate "no!" It sees only betrayal in its natural desires. The "No" is sustained in our acts; and through it, our fidelity to God is maintained.

Something very similar also occurs in prayer; but here the enterprise is one of more vast dimensions. It is not just a morally reprehensible object that temptingly offers itself to us. All creatures of whatever sort become an obstacle. We must overcome their attraction in order to be with God. Our difficulties generally spring from the fact that we do not sufficiently mistrust ourselves. Under the pretext that the things that come to our mind are neither wicked nor forbidden in themselves, we easily believe that we are committing no wrong when we are concerned with them from one end to the other of our prayer. It is this that deludes us. We have never succeeded in putting ourselves in God's presence; between Him and us is a solid wall of attachment to creatures which divert us from His love.

Considered from this point of view, the most dangerous creatures are not those which are an occasion of sin. We know quite clearly that under pain of committing sin we must sever ourselves from them. The dangerous ones are precisely those which we are duty-bound to love—and to love dearly. These constitute the greatest obstacle to prayer because they are at bottom only creatures, no matter how sacred a place they have in our hearts, and they can never be anything else but obstacles to perfect union with God. It is of course no sin to think about them. It is right, exceedingly right and proper for us to do so. The question, however, is whether they are loved in God; whether they will force God out of the only place He will accept in our minds and in our hearts during our prayer.

Hence our loved ones must be provisionally set aside—with even greater vigilance because of their very goodness and the good they do for us. St. Catherine of Sienna, who had a truly exquisite feeling for friendship, once advised St. Raymond of Capua to cut himself off from every creature, from herself first of all. The fact was that she was very attached to Raymond and he to her—both of them enjoyed each other's friendship up to the end of their lives. But in the life of prayer the very least we can do is to let God be the only occupant of our souls. This is the price of putting ourselves in His presence, of making any intimate contact with Him.

Prayer is thus the loftiest exercise conceivable in terms of valor and courage. It requires a vitality ceaselessly renewed throughout our entire being. There was an old regulation in the French Cavalry which has an important lesson for us in this respect: "Throw your heart over the obstacle and your horse will follow it." Here the obstacle is the whole universe. We must throw our hearts as far as possible, beyond the entire world and even the peaks of heaven, right up to the throne of God Himself.

Prayer is the shadow of death falling over our souls. "For though I should walk in the midst of the shadow of death, I will fear no evils for thou art with me."

God is with us only if we have first consented to walk in this awesome shadow of death. We put ourselves in the presence of God as if we were dying. To die is to give up one's soul. Prayer too is a severance of the soul from everything;

from selfhood first of all in order to deliver it up to the hands of Him of whom St. Paul has written: "It is a terrible thing to fall into the hands of the living God." Indeed it is the moment to muster up all one's courage. A six year old boy once said to me: "I never retreat." "So you have never been scared?" I asked him. "O yes, I get scared," he told me, "but when I'm scared I advance all the more rapidly."

Prayer is truly the shadow of death: it assumes all its forms and exigencies. Christians are accustomed to say of a person who has just died, that *he has appeared before his Maker*. This expression is tantamount to "let us put ourselves in the presence of God." This is the reason, furthermore, why the ancient Jews clearly perceived that no one could see God without first dying. They were right. We do not enter into God's presence without first dying. The severance that death effects is prefigured in the radical severance that prayer imposes. We are forced to leave behind external goods, friends, those who are dearest to us. Then the body itself darkens and grows cold; we take leave of it, so to speak. The soul is delivered up to the unknown, cast down from its heights into the dizzying depths of the beyond. Prayer too requires such death and in prayer we must resolve to effect all these severances willingly. We must turn away our affections from all objects, as we do in the act of dying. If saints die so easily, it is because they have acquired the habit of dying, so to speak, by praying with all their might for so long a time. Doing it once more appears to them just a trifling matter.

It is as hard or as easy, whichever you wish, to pray as it is to die. But the kingdom of God is only for those who can take it violently, by storm. Most people prefer anything else rather than surrendering to this violent severance from selfhood and from all attachment to creatures. It would be much easier to find people prepared to spend whole nights at the bedside of the sick rather than willingly face the effort required to put themselves in the presence of God—with all the generosity and sacrifice that it involves. This, nevertheless, is what is required of us. There are only two sorts of souls in the world: those who pray, and those who do not pray at all or do so badly. These latter have never consented to sacrificing those whom they love for the duration of their prayers. Such persons are at the mercy of the world which they never want to leave.

Considered in this light, prayer is obviously no easy task. But this is just one more reason for us to persevere in prayer. If we experience a great pleasure, as sometimes happens, an agreeable and intimate pleasure during prayer, we no longer know very clearly why we are praying. We do not know whether we are praying to God in order to draw nearer to Him or for our own pleasure and personal satisfaction. Joy in prayer can be sweet to the heart. It consoles us for many of the sacrifices made. But when prayer offers us no tangible satisfaction, and when we find that prayer engenders only a feeling of aridity and a kind of dark despair but we persist in prayer nonetheless, searching for God alone across this wasteland, rejecting even our own bitter sadness, then we are quite sure that we are actually praying to God in order to find Him. For no earthly personage could impose on us such a harsh and desolate period of waiting. We would never endure it save for the hope that God, the presence of God, is at the end of our long vigil.

We must possess not only a manner or style of praying but we must also devote the necessary time to it. We could easily delude ourselves over an axiom like the following: "Prayer is necessary to Christian life." We could easily believe that we have discharged our obligations with a few vocal prayers that are recited for whatever they may be worth. Such an axiom has a practical meaning and it is valid only under certain conditions just as the following axiom, for example applies in very precise circumstances: "In order for a boat to move forward, it must be in water." Were I to amuse myself by taking cupfuls of water and emptying them under a boat, there would be water under the boat but not enough to raise it and let it sail off. A definite amount of water is required, "a definite draught," i.e., the amount of water that a boat draws or displaces. The same applies to the soul. In order for the soul to be lifted and borne towards God, it requires a definite amount of prayer, a definite "draught" of prayer. The deeper and broader the prayer, the lighter and swifter will be the soul's pursuit of its God. On the other hand, a paltry prayer, mere cupfuls of it will leave the soul inert, cumbersome, and make spiritual progress impossible. Prayer must lay siege to the soul with deep, lashing waves in order to lead it back, in one instant and forever, towards the open sea.

It is remarkable indeed that the first part of the "Our Father" should be totally concerned with God and nothing else. These first petitions are the most beautiful and the most efficacious expression of the act of putting ourselves in the presence of God.

Our Father. Our feeling that we are the offspring of God gives us the taste and the boldness for prayer. We present ourselves before God like a hungry child who asks his father for something to eat. Will He give us a serpent?

Who art in heaven. We are invited to join with God where He dwells, not among the things of the world, among objects that are naturally within our reach, but in a region above and beyond every created thing. We can join with God immediately in His heaven by severance from selfhood which the effort of prayer effects in us and by the vitality with which it imbues us.

Hallowed be Thy name. An individual's name is what distinguishes Him from all the others, what He himself holds most dear because it expresses his identity. His name and his honor are one and the same. To wish that the name of God be hallowed is to wish that God's identity be recognized. It is to wish to honor Him in Himself and consequently to make available to Him the place that is His due, to adore Him resolutely and completely. The name of God must be hallowed, i.e., distinguished and separated from all others in the act of homage. It is the only name to be adored among all names. Prayer is this total homage.

Thy kingdom come. The kingdom of God is first of all this absolute dominion over the soul—through the free consent of all the faculties to the supernatural obedience of faith and charity. May this kingdom come, may this dominion extend everywhere, may it subject all other dominions to it, may it gently and firmly bend all of them to its will, may it make them bloom in the fecundity of the Cross. May this kingdom come even, and especially, into our souls and hearts. May God take our souls into His hands, may He do with them as He wills. Our soul, then, will no longer be able to disobey God. It will be inside the kingdom, as though hidden in a maternal womb, sustained and formed by His divine dominion over it.

Thy will be done. It is by doing the will of God that we can prove our love for Him. When we love God, we do what He wills. That is the way His kingdom lives. We ourselves are not at all an object of concern in these initial petitions of the *Pater*. They revolve only around God, His name, His kingdom, His will. There is no turning to anything that is not God. There is not even any explicit concern with our salvation. These things will come as a natural result: "Seek first the kingdom of God and His justice, and all these things shall be given you besides." The *Our Father* is not even concerned with the most legitimate things, such as supernatural graces for us. If we seek the sanctification of the name of God, the advent of His kingdom, the performance of His will with utter purity, vigorously and with all our heart, the rest will indeed come as a natural result, including our eternal salvation and all the graces necessary for us in this world. Hence let us desire the consummation of this lofty will of God—as it exists in itself, still unknown to us, hidden in the mystery of the heart of God, this will that is unfathomable in relation to all our foresights and all our desires, this will which (because it is divine) surpasses our understanding from all sides. It would not be divine if it did do this. Let us rest in peace; we know that our fate is in the hands of Another. Let us trust God that this will, which is God's, is benevolent, indeed exceedingly so because it is His. He cannot but will our good, because He is our Father and His good is ours.

Above all let us not put our narrow desires in the place of God's will. Let us accept this will of God in advance, from the beginning of all our prayers. Let us accept it in all its incomprehensibility and with all its hazards. Let us actualize this will little by little, tentatively groping our way in proportion as we perceive its mysterious concatenation. Let us achieve it like a blind person weaves a net, carefully choosing every mesh, but never knowing where he actually is with it. In doing God's will on earth in this way His name is really glorified. We do not betray it; we pledge our loyalty on earth to God and to a will which is not of the earth. This latter note will always make God's work wear a strange countenance. It will appear (so to speak) like a mendicant passing by, one with whom we are not acquainted and who strikingly demands from us everything we have.

It is only after we have dwelt on what exclusively concerns God that we are authorized by the *Pater* to ask something for ourselves or for others. In order to pray well, we must set aside everything which is not God. If we employ formulas, we must never become their dupes, but make use of them in order to penetrate them; and by means of them, to plunge into the depths of the heart of God. This is why it is important to use very simple formulas and particularly consecrated formulas like that of the *Pater*, to persevere in them and to repeat them slowly, pondering every word. With a purity of intention that is as perfect as possible we must desire nothing else but God, His kingdom, His will, the sanctification of His name. When we do that, we are the master of our prayer; but in that very instant prayer actually takes possession of us and carries us off to the deep recesses of divine union.

We must first of all seek God even when we pray for others. May His will be done in all, for all and by all. To pray for someone is to love him in the presence of God. To love him, i.e., to wish him good and especially that good above all other goods which is eternal life: the performance of the will of God now and forever. In order to love others rightly, the important thing is to be in the presence of God. We must live in the presence of God, plunge ourselves in it, in order to love others in a Christian manner. We do good to others only to the degree that we are united not with them, but with God. It is only when we are hidden in the recesses of God's heart that we shall have the power to procure for our loved ones the goods that we desire for them.

The second part of the *Pater*, moreover, never disassociates us from others. What we petition is always for *us*. The things we ask for, we request in the plural and without the slightest exception. First of all we ask for our daily bread for *this* day. God undoubtedly wants us to be satisfied with what is sufficient for us. We are invited to be as fastidious about our bread as fashionable folk who would never have a day-old roll with their morning coffee. This petition, moreover, does not assume its full significance unless by *daily bread* we mean first the grace of God and the gifts of the Holy Spirit—things which will no more be refused to us than one refuses bread to hungry children. But in petitioning God for His love we must ask for it in terms of its daily character. We must ask only for the grace of this day—strength for the present moment. All this is quite consistent with the nature of things, moreover: the fact that we are children who ask, the fact that God will give to His children only the grace of the present moment, and the fact that normally it does not occur to the mind of children to demand a week's food supply in advance.

This latter thought would particularly strike them as absurd. Nobody goes to the bakery to buy bread for three weeks. We know very well that this bread would become stale and inedible, and we trust that the bakery will still be open three weeks hence. Let us at least have the same trust in Providence. When we eat, we know that it is only for the present day, that tomorrow we shall again feel the pangs of hunger and that we shall again need something to eat. To be hungry is just a sign of health. We have trust in the morrow that will bring its nourishment to the measure of our hunger. Little children do not worry about it and neither should we. They leave the worrying to their parents; similarly we know that the grace we have for today is enough for us, that the strength which God gives us today allows us to hold out for now. Tomorrow we will have a dispensation of grace to the measure of our hunger, a strength equal to the dimensions of our task.

With God we can be sure that the table is always set. If we pray, we may be sure we will lack nothing. It would be an act of insolence to accept an invitation and, on arriving at our host's house ask him for a guarantee about all the meals that we are to take at his table. We are with God in life and in death. What must disappoint Him, so to speak, is that we frequently behave like ill-mannered children.

"A certain man gave a great supper, and he invited many. And he sent his servant at supper time to tell those invited to come, for everything is now ready.

And they all with one accord began to excuse themselves. The first said to him, 'I have bought a farm, and I must go out and see it; I pray thee, hold me excused.'

And another said, 'I have bought five yoke of oxen, and I am on my way to try them; I pray thee, hold me excused.'

And another said, 'I have married a wife, and therefore I cannot come.'

And the servant returned, and reported these things to his master. Then the master of the house was angry and said to his servant, 'Go out quickly into the streets and lanes of the city and bring in here the poor, and the crippled, and the blind, and the lame . . . For I tell you that none of those who were invited shall taste of my supper.' "

The banquet is communion with God in prayer. No one will be able to excuse himself. All of us must participate in it. There is no valid excuse to dispense with prayer. All the arguments set forth by the invited guests are excellent. There is nothing wrong in what they do: it is quite proper, moreover, to have bought a field and to busy oneself with it, to try out a pair of oxen and to go on a honeymoon. But the master of the house is justifiably annoyed in the context of our Lord's parable; for prayer is not just one obligation among others. It does not prevent us from working the fields, or leading oxen, or from marrying. But we must learn how to perform these legitimate tasks in the larger pattern of Divine Love.

Nothing can dispense us from prayer: it is the most fundamental exercise of the love of God. Whether we be poor, blind, crippled, it does not matter. So let us approach God with what we have, with nothing if that is the case, as paupers, as mendicants. Let us approach God gropingly if we do not see, like blind men. Let us approach God hobbling, limping, if we walk badly, or like cripples. But let us get up and go forth to meet Him, and let us not halt until we have united ourselves with His Love.

I Will Dwell Among Them

DOES God dwell anyplace where we may go and live with Him and unite ourselves to Him?

God is of course present everywhere through His creative action. All things derive their being as well as their continuation in being from Him. If God were (so to speak) to close His eyes, the world would disappear. His is a sovereign presence, a dominion which embraces everything without exception, a total suzerainty which is exercised even over demons and encircles the very fabric of all that stands outside of nothingness. But this immensity, in revealing God to us, simultaneously hides Him from us. This omnipresence, by making us constantly come up against God, obscures Him from us. Through it we discover God only from the outside; the little that we do apprehend of Him makes us worship Him as the fearsome Lord who inhabits an inaccessible light. We are engulfed with fear at the thought of His perfections which are as real as they are eminent; but their very eminence constitutes a barrier obscuring the divine mystery.

Are we, then, supposed to extend our arms hopelessly towards an unfeeling heaven, to cry out to Someone who will not answer, to erect an altar on our Acropolae to an unknown God? "He is not far from any one of us," said St. Paul to the philosophers of Athens, "for in Him we live and move and have our being, as indeed some of your own poets have said. *For we also are His offspring.*"

We are immersed in God's immensity, but if we want to discover His adorable countenance more exactly, let us look into this mirror of our own nativity. There we shall find God in the same way that we recognize the father in the son.

We are in fact God's offspring. It is undeniably true that man carries in himself a likeness to God that makes him a ruler over the earth, that places creation prostrate at his feet. "Let us make man to our image and likeness and let him have dominion," said God. This God is everywhere—in all things. But when likeness is raised to the level of kinship, as it undoubtedly is in man's spirit, is it not present in a different and more perfect manner in a creature in whom it has been especially brought to completion?

God is Truth and Love and Spirit. Man is like Him in the sense that he too possesses intelligence to perceive truth; and a will which represents the spiritual gravitation of the mind. This intellectual nature of man is an image of God and in a special way, theologians tell us, of the Trinity.

It is hardly possible for us to approach God more closely than by way of this image and it is this to which Jesus often referred, particularly on Holy Thursday when the stars blazed in the sky like lamps of love, as they are described in the *Canticle of Canticles.* He said: "If anyone love me, he will keep my word and my Father will love him, and we will come to him and make our abode with him." We ourselves are the house of God. Such is the universal law of Christianity: our souls are an image which blooms into a real presence.

Without being paradoxical, we may say that the beginning of the presence of God in us is precisely His absence. "Man is a religious animal," say the sociologists; and the formula is a good one, insofar as it affirms that the natural requirements of our minds predispose us towards God. It is in a negative and evasive manner that we conceive God as different from all that which environs us, as the necessary perfection of an imperfect world, singularly like the essentially hypothetical consummation we conceive of our own nature. This does not of course prove that there is a God; or that we can share in His life, but it does underline a human wish to see God, a capacity for divine life which already constitutes for us an absence. This absence suggests a possible presence; this empty place invites us to await the mysterious guest who, perhaps at this very moment, is seating Himself beside us, as the wayside traveller once did at the inn at Emmaus. "Here I am. I stand at the door and knock. If anyone hears my voice and opens the door to me, I shall enter his house, and I shall sup with him, and he with me." This is the scriptural image of an eternal banquet with divinity where, in the mystery of contemplation and of prayer and later in the glory of a face-to-face encounter, we are called to enjoy the presence of the Lord, to nourish ourselves from His substance.

All the fruits of the earth will leave us eternally unsatisfied. Whether we wish it or not, ever since God willed to effect an encounter with us, the demands of our own destiny catapult us into His presence. If we reject Him as a friend, we shall still have to come face to face with Him as a judge. Moreover, He does not impose Himself on us by fear. He desires to be loved freely. Unbelievers ought to pay attention to this much at least, that their doubt may be a secret stimulus to prayer, a wedge which their souls force into the unknown, an anguished cry to God to manifest His presence to them. What do they risk if God does not exist? In this night of their solitude there is nothing else that would give them an eternal answer. "Ask and it shall be given you; seek and you shall find; knock and it shall be opened to you."

Our appeals to God are not in vain. His is a wordless voice, an extraordinary voice, yet one that is already recognized, that is as familiar as a friendship, that penetrates to the center of the soul. "Fear not, it is I. I am with you. Turn not away. I am your God. I have already been your comfort and your succour. Without you noticing it, the right hand of my Just One has seized you. Resist not this hand, wounded for your love.

I am the Lord your God. I have called you by your name. You are mine."

God makes Himself recognized as God and as possessed by the soul in one stroke: "My soul," said the Psalmist "hath desired thee in the night: yea, and with my spirit within me in the morning early I will watch to thee . . . for thy dew is the dew of the light. . . . The night of my doubt and yearning is lit with hope."

God is absolutely incompatible with all things other than Himself. He is a fire devouring all that is not Himself; He remains inaccessible to mere flesh and blood. Except for our call to the life of grace, it would be an intolerable presumption on the part of a creature to wish to love God in Himself. For to see God or to love God, must not one already be God—either by nature or by real adoption?

Through grace we human beings have a participation in divine nature. The least amount of this grace is more precious than the whole world.

"I the Lord, am your God, your Savior. You have assumed honor and glory in my eyes. I have loved you. Shall I give people in exchange for you and nations in exchange for your soul? Fear not, I am with you." In the eyes of God, only God matters. If we begin to assume value in His eyes, it is because we are His offspring. Grace is a new birth for us, introducing us to a wholly new life. "Amen, amen, I say to you, unless a man be born again, he cannot see the kingdom of God . . . that which is born of the flesh is flesh, and that which is born of the Spirit is spirit. . . . And no one knows the Father except him who has descended from heaven, the Son of Man who is in heaven."

There is a legend that Origen's father bent over his newly baptized infant, and lovingly worshipped him like a tabernacle of the living God. In reality, without knowing it yet, every baptized child is in the state of grace and sleeps in paradise. He is borne on the heart of God, rocked in his fatherly arms. He must only awaken to a consciousness of himself in order for him to be able to love this embrace.

Poor human creatures that we are, overtaken suddenly by the Spirit, enclosed in a mysterious gestation that kneads us like dough, repairs us and restores us from top to bottom, infuses us with a mystic blood: eternity flows in our souls and leads us with miraculous energy into the regions of which we ourselves will never be aware. "The kingdom of God is like the leaven that a diligent housewife buries in three measures of flour until everything is leavened." Divine grace is a leaven which monopolizes all the dough of the spirit, raises it, permeates it, fructifies the faculties, and elevates them to a supernatural life that is the very life of God. In these three measures, the Fathers gladly recognized an image of the human soul as well as confirmation of their belief that the soul is by nature a likeness of the Holy Trinity.

An image, yes; but it is an image that is by nature obscure, and one that is still disfigured by the taint of sin. It is a living mirror, but one that is immersed in darkness and ignorance. May the eternal morning dawn and the sun of justice rise in all its strength over us! But this wretched, darkened mirror must be cleansed of all earthly dust in order to sustain the brilliance of such splendor. "It is necessary," says Ruysbroeck, "that either the spirit ever be in the likeness of God by means of grace and virtues, or that it be unlike Him through the fact of mortal sin. For if man is made in the likeness of God, this means that he is made to receive His grace, since grace is a God-forming light that penetrates us with its rays and endows us with the divine likeness. We could not be united with God supernaturally without this light which gives us this similitude. Although the image that is within us and the natural unity with God cannot be lost, we shall be damned if we lose the divine likeness that comes through grace. Thus, from the moment that God finds us receptively disposed to His grace, He is induced by His gratuitous goodness to vivify us, to make us like unto Him. He imprints His image and His likeness on us, unbosoming Himself with His gifts. He delivers us from our sins, liberates us and makes us like unto Him. . . . Then, with this same divine action which erases our sins and gives us likeness and freedom in charity, the spirit itself is immersed in a love of fruition. Then an encounter and a union is effected where dwells our loftiest beatitude, supernaturally and without any intermediary."

Spirit constitutes a unique order in the universe. While remaining substantially the same, it possesses the faculty of becoming something else, of assimilating itself to an object outside itself, of existing beyond its physical existence in another existence which it causes to be its own, of appropriating a nature different from itself without violating its diversity. The spirit becomes the "other" as "other." Through knowledge, everything belongs to it. In its transparency it is capable of reflecting everything with an intensity so total that its specific perfection as spirit is to be identified absolutely with the known object, as though devoured by it. Therefore this assimilation is a veritable presence of the object at the center of the knowing mind. When we comprehend something—*comprehendere*, i.e. grasp or catch hold of it mentally—we usually say, "Now it's clear in my mind." No longer is it a juxtaposition of two essentially different natures, but a mutual interpenetration in the order peculiar to the activity of the spirit, an intimate fusion, the flowering of that which is known and loved into the spirit of him who knows and loves.

Another quality peculiar to the spirit is a capacity to effect a severance from self in order to deliver self up to another thing, to be able to project the self into another being in which it itself blooms and whose dynamism and nature it adopts. Thereby it brings about a special unity with its object, a unity that is peculiarly spiritual, greater than the union of the soul and body, i.e. absolute identity in the intentional order.

With regard to the supernatural order, its especially privileged character consists in the fact that God, the object of knowledge, is at the same time the first cause and the ontological root of the knowing subject. As such He already exists in the soul by His presence of immensity—a presence that is creative and preservative of everything that exists. But this immensity binds us to God in a manner that is external to Him, even though the bond is to our innermost recesses: it makes us orbit around His universal attraction. All that is ours is God's first of all: the immensity of God in relation to us is nothing else but a servitude which puts us under His obligation, a divine proprietary title He has to all that we are. But no matter how great a philosopher one might be, this presence of immensity teaches us nothing about the mysteries of divine life.

And Jesus said: "No longer do I call you servants, because the servant does not know what his master does. But I have called you friends, because all things that I have learned from my Father I have made known to you."

If we consider grace only as a raw and created effect of God, it does not cause God to be present to us in any way other than His immensity. But viewed in terms of its essential thrust, its irresistable effort, its divine impetuosity, grace forces the gates of brass and bursts the bars of iron guarding the mysteries of God. For the reason that it is for God, it joyously flows into God, it hides us in the very bosom of the Trinity. Indeed, this is the effect peculiar to it: this penetration it makes to the very center of God, this friendship by which the soul is introduced to the intimacy of God as though it were at home, this aptitude to fathom God Himself who gives us the Three Divine Persons as our very own, even to the point that we enjoy them because they are ours and we dispose of their life. Their life is our life.

Our association with them is entirely heavenly;

it is constituted in the heavens. Our human soul becomes a fountain of love which gushes forth in the heart of God. "Now, on the last, the great day of the feast, Jesus stood and cried out, saying 'If anyone thirst, let him come to me and drink. He who believes in me . . . from within him there shall flow rivers of living water.' " St. John adds: "He said this, however, of the Spirit whom they who believed in Him were to receive."

It may have been only a moment ago that God's omnipresence touched us in a dominating contact of suzerainty which, by exhausting our being at its wonder and immensity, hid God from us and isolated Him in His glory. Once there is an infusion of grace, however, behold how God opens Himself to us and how He takes us into His confidence. Astounded in the bottomless depth of the waters of its life, the illuminated spirit siezes upon Him from whom it has everything: this omnipresent Being of whom it was ignorant, this God who was immense and distant until then but who, not content with granting it being and action, offers Himself to it further as a object of enjoyment, as the bread of the supernatural life, in order to assimilate it to Himself and to let it become God, to participate in the divine nature.

This contact with God is at root an act of knowledge, a penetration of an intentional order. Here, however, the divine object is no longer known as separated but as present, newly present as a friend at the center of the soul which he vivifies. To enjoy an object is to possess it. Hence this knowledge of God as non-distant, as possessed; this enjoyment of Him that grace makes available to us, are a new mode of the divine presence grafted on the presence of immensity. God, essentially present but hidden from our eyes, has suddenly revealed Himself to us. From now on we can contemplate Him or, rather, obscurely savor Him, and discern by touch (so to speak) the lineaments of His living reality.

And He Himself gives us the fruition of His

creative countenance. God, we formerly believed, is too immense, too great, too distant, too high above us in the heavens. But suddenly, God is there! His greatness is a presence which impregnates us. His remoteness is a sublimity which governs us. His prodigious loftiness is a profundity of love. And this God, at the center of our souls, offers Himself to the loving experience of the believer. Awesome indeed is this palace of our souls! "This is really the house of God and the gate of heaven. Surely the Lord inhabits this place, He pours forth His glory there and we did not know it." Hence the unprecedented significance that the promises of Isaiah take on: "And I will give thee hidden treasures and the concealed riches of secret places that thou mayest know that I am the Lord who calls thee by thy name." And there is another text of resplendent precision: "*Assimilavi te*! I have assimilated thee, I bear thee within myself, thou livest of my life, I am the soul of thy soul, I have renewed thee in me, thou art in me and of me, like a child borne in its mother's womb."

"And he who was sitting on the throne said, 'Behold I make all things new.' And he said, 'Write, for these words are trustworthy and true.' And he said to me, 'It is done! I am the Alpha and Omega, the beginning and the end. To him who thirsts I will give the fountain of the water of life, freely. He who overcomes shall possess these things and I will be his God and he shall be my son.'"

It is in terms of this illumination that the requirements of prayer and the patience of the saints must be judged. Whatever the tribulations of this world may be, they are disproportionate to the glory that will one day be revealed in us. It is certainly worthwhile to endure a spiritual combat here below—even though it may be much more brutal than all the battles of men. In it we can always draw nearer to God "with the step of love", penetrate even further the mystery of His ardent visage, hide ourselves ever more deeply in His light, like grasshoppers in the sun.

"Dominus vobiscum!" God is reborn in us with His own life. The word of the priest, like that which the angel addressed to the Virgin, is an annunciation at the same time as it is an invitation, an assurance of mystic but real presence, just as at Nazareth it was the promise of an unprecedented and unique Incarnation. Thus the mystical body of Christ is conceived by the *Fiat* of love, and the strength of the Holy Spirit covered us with His shadow: "For you are the temple of the living God; and as God says, 'I will dwell and move among them. I will be their God and they shall be my people. . . .' Having therefore these promises," continues the Apostle, "let us cleanse ourselves of all defilements of the flesh and of the spirit, perfecting holiness in the fear of God."

God fulfills His promises by making ceaseless

visitations to the just soul. Therein He renews the event of His sublime generation and the rich flowing of His infinite love. The divine generation, which terminates eternally in the Person of the Word, is terminated in the sphere of time in the mission of this same Word in a sanctified soul. The procession, which the Holy Spirit constitutes in His holy Personality has a temporal end in us, in sanctification of our souls.

A soul in the state of grace knows God through His word and loves Him through His Spirit. God is born in the soul at each new instant. The Holy Spirit pours all His gifts into it. The soul is immersed, submerged in the streams of divine life. There the soul escapes into a wisdom and a love which no longer bear the marks of any terrestrial thing: the soul dwells in God, it enjoys Him, it savors Him, it delectably nourishes itself on Him. In familiar intimacy with God, and inside the mysterious exchanges of divine life between the Three Persons, the soul experiences a close union with the Word Incarnate.

Obscurely, but in a real sense, the soul feels itself to be the beloved child of the Father, the temple of the Holy Spirit. It is a wondrous filiation, a mystical nuptial, a total dedication of the soul to the Holy Spirit—and one which raises the Christian to the dizzying heights of the Trinity.

Such delights are essentially imperceptible to a natural sensibility. They appertain only to the life of faith; and it is interesting to note that they can coexist with feelings of despair or anxiety. What need do I have of a God cut to my measure, one with whom I would naturally be on an equal footing, a God on my level, as inferior as myself?

"*But we speak the wisdom of God, mysterious, hidden, which God foreordained before the world unto our glory, a wisdom which none of the rulers of this world has known. . . . Eye has not seen, nor ear heard, nor has it entered into the heart of man to conceive what things God has prepared for those who love Him. But to us God has revealed them through His Spirit. For the Spirit searches all things, even the deep things of God. For who among men knows the things of a man save the spirit of the man which is in him? Even so, the things of God no one knows but the Spirit of God. Now we have received not the spirit of the world, but the spirit that is from God, that we may know the things that have been given us by God."*

Such an incomplete and obscure knowledge is only a meager and provisional taste of the purely spiritual nourishment which satiates the angels and for which we hunger. The soul endures a great labor of love which increases its hunger, all the while giving it a more concrete enticement to the great banquet of God's kingdom. Before the eyes of the believing heart, consolation, peace, joy, riches, beauty, all that which gives birth to happiness are found in God without measure. Such a taste of God makes one desire death in order to see. "Whoever does not desire to die," says Bossuet "is not a Christian."

One would have to fathom God in order to evaluate the perfection of a soul which has known how to make such ascents to God in its heart. "The soul," says Ruysbroeck, "is lost to itself in an absence of moods and in a darkness in which all contemplative minds are fruitfully sunken, incapable of ever finding themselves again. It is in the depths of this darkness, where the loving spirit is dead to itself, that the revelation of God and life begin, eternally. *All the riches that are in God by nature, we possess in Him through love*, and God possesses us in Himself through the immense Love which is the Holy Spirit, for in this love we savor all we can desire."

Just as God is neither wisdom, nor truth, nor goodness, nor this, nor that, but in an absolute sense identifies all perfections in His eminent and infinitely sovereign simplicity, likewise the saint is neither maganimous, nor humble, nor meek, nor strong, nor just, nor merciful: he is all these but in a manner peculiarly his own, a divine manner, infinitely free, unforeseeable and paradoxical. All the Christian virtues come into play in his soul and fuse exquisitely into love. As Saint Thérèse of the Infant-Jesus teaches us: "In the heart of the Church, my Mother, I shall be love, and thus I shall be all."

What we learn from such statements is that this type of soul, withdrawn from the world and transported with ecstasy to the very bosom of the Trinity, is possessed by God—to the very point that it is forgetful of everything, even of itself. It is more cut off from the whole universe than a dead person, it is a cadaver inhabited by an immense light. The impetuosity of grace in this soul would resemble a fickle rashness were it not a passionate unbridled obedience to the Spirit whom (as we know) no man can judge. Ezechiel the prophet had one such fearful vision:

"And every one of them went straight forward: where the impulse of the spirit was to go, there they went. And they turned not when they went. And as for the likeness of the living creatures, their appearance was like that of burning coals of fire, and like the appearance of lamps. This was the vision running to and fro in the midst of the living creatures, a bright fire, and lightning going forth from the fire."

This doctrine, we should note, is the very reverse of all pantheism. God is not fashioned by the soul which he inhabits. He is not the result of a natural religiosity. No matter how intelligent, how refined, how broadminded we might be, how favored we might be with gifts of mind and heart, no matter what generosity and nobility we might possess, such gifts will never of themselves introduce us into the presence and friendship of God, if God does not make the first advance towards us, if He does not first open the path towards us by granting us His forgiveness and grace. In all circumstances, it is God who is the first to love and who gives access to all familiarity with Him.

And the presence of God in the soul always preserves the character of a free encounter on the part of God—one which fills the soul with dread at seeing God lovingly stoop to our wretchedness. Without any injustice toward us, God could have locked Himself up in His joy. Nor is there any absorption of two essences in one. In heaven, the beatified intelligence will immediately flower into the Word, and the Holy Spirit will be the fruit of our beatitude. But the substance of God will not remain less infinitely distinct and separated from all other creatures—entirely untouched in His Infinite Reality. This substance will be revealed to the blessed without undergoing the slightest change even of the most fleeting character.

This is easy to understand. Even in the sensory order, the sight of a tree changes nothing about the tree. But the fact that we see it is very real. In a similar way the blessed will behold God as He is; the vision will transform them without annihilating their nature: on the contrary, it will complement nature in a wonderful way. But what God was in the beginning, He will remain forever, *in saecula saeculorum*, world without end. He will be the joy of His elect, without His infinite beatitude undergoing the slightest diminution or increase: an ocean of peace, of light and of happiness, radiant and ever tranquil.

We shall one day know God fully, as He knows Himself. We shall be like Him. Just as in the simplicity of His act, He is Identically knowing subject and known object, likewise in an absolute self-transparency, He will simultaneously be the object of our vision and the light that makes us see. At the roots of our being, He will still be the total cause of our intellectual nature and of its operation. But the image we are will have flowered into a reality. God will be all in all. This sweet country will be filled with the knowledge of the Lord as are the depths of the seas by the waters that cover them. The Church will complete her unity, and like the queen Esther, after she had crossed all the threshholds of the King's house, she will behold the King Himself in His beauty.

Esther, we will recall, robed herself in all her glory.

"And glittering in royal robes she took two maids with her, and upon one of them she leaned, as if for the sake of delicacy and tenderness she were not able to bear up her own body. And the other maid followed her, bearing up her train that was flowing on the ground. But she with a rosy color in her face and with gracious and bright eyes, had a mind full of anguish, and exceeding great fear. So going on she passed through all the doors in order and stood before the king, where he sat upon his royal throne, clothed with his royal robes, and glittering with gold and precious

stones, and he was terrible to behold. And when he had lifted up his countenance, and with burning eyes had shewn the wrath of his heart, the queen sunk down, and her color turned pale, and she rested her weary head upon her handmaid. . . . In haste and in fear he leaped from his throne and held her up in his arms, till she came to herself, and caressed her with these words: What is the matter, Esther? I am thy brother, fear not. . . . Come near then, and touch the scepter. . . . And as she held her peace, he took the golden scepter, and laid it upon her neck, and kissed her and said: Why dost thou not speak to me? She answered: I saw thee my Lord, as an angel of God, and my heart was troubled for fear of thy majesty for thou, my Lord, art very admirable, and thy face is full of graces."

Bearing Witness to the Truth

When we bend over a cradle to look at a new-born infant, a tiny and wrinkled and snug little body which fidgets so amusingly but which we know contains an immortal soul still slumbering somewhere beneath its flesh, some disturbing questions frequently rise in our minds: *What will this child be? What fate awaits him in the world? What will be this child's mission or role in life?*

Questions also come to mind as we kneel before the manger on Christmas day, but there is an important difference. On Christmas a song breaks forth in all the Churches inviting Christians to a crib where a very tiny child sleeps on a patch of straw between an ox and an ass. *Puer natus est nobis. A child has been born to us.* The birth of a Child-God in the middle of the night also poses questions for us to ponder; but they are altogether different from those that arise at the birth of other human beings.

In moments of despair, as though it were an evil prompting of the devil, a cry sometimes bursts from the depths of our desolation. "After all, I didn't ask to be born and to live!" But Jesus Christ asked to be born and to live. Let us look at the Infant Jesus in His crib: here he is among us like one of us, yet He is foreordained to suffering, to anxiety, to tears, to death. He was God and therefore nothing was lacking to Him. It was not necessary for Him to come into the world. It would not have made any difference to Him if He were not born a man. He was under no obligation to be born in this valley of tears. But He chose to do this freely and He prepared everything beforehand in order to do it well: the time, the place, His race and His Mother. The question this child poses to the mind is not:

"What will become of Him?", but rather, "Why did He do this?"

Jesus Himself has replied to this question. In order to give a more solemn character to His declaration, He chose the moment when He was officially condemned to death at Pilate's tribunal to explain His birth and His coming into the world. From the moment of His mysterious birth, this Child, in the arms of His mother, a poor young girl resplendent with her purity, was a *witness*. Throughout His entire life, among the offspring of men, He will bear witness to the truth.

What is a witness? He is a person who is perfectly informed about a matter of which others are ignorant. He reveals this hidden matter and he furnishes its proof by the authority of his word. Nothing is more just than to say of the Infant Jesus that He is a witness and that His temporal birth has put Him in a position to bear witness to Himself. The truth to which He has come to bear witness and which has been hidden from our minds, is God Himself—Truth subsisting in the excellence of His intimate nature, the ineffable society of the Father and of the Son and of the Holy Spirit, equal in power and in majesty in the single divine substance, revealing itself to our intelligence in faith, giving itself to our souls through charity, and associating us eternally to the divine beatitude: *God with us, God for us.*

Three qualities are required of a witness.

The first is that the witness thoroughly know what he is talking about. Who can bear witness to God, so withdrawn in an inaccessible light and in the inviolable mystery of His silence, this unknown God of whom St. John has said, "No one has at any time seen God?" But he added: "The only-begotten Son who is in the bosom of the Father, he has revealed him." One must be God in order to know God as He is and to talk about Him. This Child is God Himself by nature, God in His substantive revelation, the King of the Angels who will subjugate heaven, earth and hell through His miracles, who will forgive men their sins and who will rise from the grave through His own power. This Child who sleeps in a feeding trough for animals is not only a messenger for God, or His mere Representative, or His Prophet; He is His son: not a son of an inferior and adoptive status, but His natural Son, equal to the Father, Himself substantially God, and there is no God outside of Him; God in the plenitude and the rich flowing of His glory. An angel would not be enough to teach us what God is, nor would all the philosophers put together. With regard to such lofty truths as these, we would have difficulty believing angels or philosophers.

It is the Child who does what no one else can do, who stirs us so deeply and convinces us of the truth and of the love of God. By Himself He is the proof of what He affirms. Indeed He Himself is an ineluctable affirmation of the love of

God, of the gift of God and of His revelation. Jesus is the manifestation of God: His epiphany, God loving us and disclosing Himself to us, God become ours. God is no longer the immense—but how abstract!—being of the philosophers. He is no longer the harsh lawgiver of the Jews who wrote His commandments on stone and bent rebelious necks under His inflexible yoke. Our Christian God is God-become-man: born in innocence of an innocent virgin, a source of terror to demons, but helpful and compassionate towards sinners. He is a God who is very near and familiar to us through His sacraments and through the Eucharist, and who brought the testimony of His divine truth to fulfillment by shedding all His blood on the cross.

Another attribute required from a witness is that he be understandable to us. Of what use will it be that I am well informed if I do not speak the same language as you? Hitherto God had chosen intermediaries in order to speak to men.

The Jews said to Moses: "Speak thou to us and we will hear. Let not the Lord speak to us, lest we die."

If one must be God in order to know God, one must be a man among men in order to speak to men. This is an amazing condition for God to express His Truth adequately, but this is what actually happened. God became man in order to make Himself as clearly understood and loved as is possible. This Child tells us who God is, by hiding the fearsome brilliance of Divine majesty under the veil of weakness. God humanized Himself. He assumed a complete human nature, a body in flesh and bones, not mere appearance like those of a phantom. He assumed an intelligent and free soul, like each one of our souls. This Child is surely our offspring. He proves it by being born of a woman. He will prove it by suffering and by dying in order to make us understand that He is God and how much He loves us. *Principium qui loquor vobis.* Yes, this Child was born expressly to tell us about God, and in

His babbling it is God who puts Himself within our reach. In this Child full of grace and truth, it is our miserable human nature which rises to the lofty level of bearing witness to God—a faithful witness to God—who is in fact identical with the real presence of what is being affirmed; God has become a Child, and this Child who slumbers in the arms of the Virgin Mary is divine Truth itself.

But the real importance of a witness lies in the dignity and authority of his person. It is precisely this which constitutes the truth of the testimony, and which in the listener's mind adjusts what is heard to what objectively exists. Should we grant so much importance to this Child's testimony? It is possible that the tribunals may reject the authority of this Child. But His person (unlike that of other children) does not await the events of later life to express itself, is not buried in the obscure imprecision of inexperience. It is already the most perfectly formed person in the world; it is characterized by supreme dignity and loftiness; it is of infinite excellence because it is divine, it is the King of all ages and all men, and it would be blasphemous to reject it. Jesus is *God in person.*

Generally, in order to give weight to his testimony, one gives his word that what he says is true. In the judgment of men of honor, such a word entirely commits a person to what he says. In order to corroborate His testimony, God has given us His word so intensely, that it is impossible for us to conceive the degree to which he has done so. He has committed Himself.

He has done so up to the uttermost limits of the gift of Himself, because Christ's word is itself divine. The word of God is the very Son of God and it is this eternal Word which possesses divine nature and human nature at once in the absolute simplicity of His personality. It is united to these two natures substantially, without either diminishing or confusing them, but perfecting each one of them. The mystery of Christ lies in this fundamental unity, despite the infinite diversity of His natures.

This unity derives wholly from the excellence of the divine Self which can appropriate a created nature and really carry on all its functions. And it can do this to the point that this Child who laughs and cries like all babies and whom a very young mother with a countenance of ineffable purity nourishes with her milk, is the Word of God inscribed in human flesh; God offering Himself and expressing Himself in a substantial sharing of the secrets of His divine nature. We have no need either of Moses, or the stone tablets of the Old Testament: how could we henceforth not understand the language of God?

Christianity is not a multiplicity of things. It is not divisible into the life of Christ born two thousand years ago in Bethlehem, who died on the cross in Jerusalem and who resurrected and ascended to the heavens; and into Christians who go to Mass on Sunday and contribute to the costs of the cult when the basket is passed around.

No, Christianity is wholly and indivisibly in Jesus. It is absolute, completed, perfectly achieved in this Child whom the Virgin Mary presents to us. One is not a Christian save to the degree to which he immediately unites in a mysteriously real way with the life of Jesus, combines with that life which alone among all lives of men is unique and sufficient unto itself. We may be excused from atending Mass on Sundays or from abstinence on Fridays for serious reasons. But the Pope himself could not exempt a Christian from believing in Jesus, from hoping in Jesus, and from uniting his heart to that Heart which is the King and Center of all the others. If we have not asked to be born, at least we surely know why we were born, why we live and why we die. God who willed to be born and to live and to die so that He might bear witness to His truth has shown us. He gives His truth to us so that we may bear the same witness—if necessary, in the shedding of blood, because "witness" means "martyr" in the original sense of the word. Our life and our death are in our hands. We can fritter both away in pure loss, uselessly and aimlessly. But would it profit us to gain the whole world, if we neglect to know, to love, and to merit God in Jesus? Life and death are given to us so that we may conform to this central mystery of Christianity: the life and death of our Lord.

Do This in Memory of Me

IN THE eleventh chapter of his Gospel, St. John records for us the words which Caiphas spoke about Christ. "It is expedient," said the High Priest, "that this one man die for the people, rather than that our nation perish." And the evangelist specifically notes that these words were said as a kind of prophecy that "Jesus was to die for the nation; and not only for the nation but that He might gather into one the children of God who were scattered abroad."

This prophetic spirit, which oriented the Hebrew priesthood and the ancient rites towards the bleeding future of the Cross, also pointed the way to the eternal priesthood and the liturgy of the new Covenant, the Mass: an indefectible memory of the sacrifice of Jesus, an exact and objective remembrance of this dolorous event which it preserves in the very act of evoking it.

Such indeed is the exact meaning of Jesus' words when He instituted the Holy Eucharist: "This cup is the new covenant in my blood which shall be shed for you. Do this in memory of me." The ancient sacraments were voided from the moment those words were expressed and the life of Christ was communicated to innumerable men and women, each of whom will be throughout the ages an instantaneous miracle of divine love. The first and immediate application of these words is of course to the ineffable reality of the martyrdom of a Man-God. But in its sacramental truth, this martyrdom was already consummated at the Last Supper under the accidents of bread and wine consecrated separately as a symbol of Christ's death, and held in Jesus holy and venerable hands. The fountains of life which on the morrow were to be the five wounds, the bloodless and lacerated body, the transfixed heart from which the Church was to gush forth, and all the other cruel and lovely mysteries of our salvation, were already really contained in this first Eucharistic Sacrifice.

Priests throughout the ages will repeat the same gestures; they will intone the same words until the end of time. The liturgical action of the Mass, on reaching the climax of the Consecration, rends the veil of the ancient temple; it joins us immediately and directly and without intermediary, with Jesus Christ the High Priest of human salvation.

Let us Christians be ever vigilant! When we attend Mass, we are present at the blessed death of our Savior Jesus Christ. This is an indisputable truth, and one which solemnly consecrates our Catholic faith, though it will always be most mysterious.

The Mass is not an empty symbol of the Cross, nor just another sacrifice in a different and simply repeated form. The Mass is the Cross itself, sacramentally elevated before the illumined eyes of our hearts; before us wretched souls, heedless or sinful, suddenly hurled at the foot of the tree of life, in whose bleeding boughs Jesus' cry of agony resounds. Christians who attend Mass should press the Cross against their breasts, like Magdalene; they should contemplate the wound of this heart like St. John; and they should commiserate this frightful execution of the most beautiful of the sons of men, like Mary, the Mother of Jesus.

"For as often as you shall eat this bread and drink of this cup, you proclaim the death of the Lord until he comes"

The Mass is this proclamation: when the body and the blood of Jesus are placed separately on the altar our salvation is consummated in plenitude and we behold our beloved Lord in the state of His redemptive death. The priest raises the

Host, then the Chalice, so all may worship this mystery. These indeed are living remembrances, remembrances carried to the extent of real presences. *For me to live is Christ.*

The memory of the Church is thus wholly concerned with the Passion of Jesus and with the Precious Blood from which she herself was born. Christ's sacrifice is the eternal treasure of the Church and of Christians—a treasure to which Christian priests hold the keys. They are annointed so that they may guard and administer this treasure, with which they seem to be identified like a mother with the child she bears. After the consecrated Host, the Priesthood of Jesus Christ seems to be what is most alive and most perfect in the world—a continuation and remembrance of Jesus Crucified.

All the members of the Church have been baptized, as St. Paul tells us, so that they may share in the sacrifice of the Cross, in the death of Jesus. Through the mediation of priests, each one receives its benefit to his measure—one five talents, another three, and another one.

Dedicated Christians would not renounce the unity of the Christian sacraments for anything in the world. But a constant association with holy things, an assiduous presence at Mass, runs the risk of making but a slight impression on our soul if we do no turn this treasure committed to our custody to profitable account. Would it still be a treasure in our eyes if we did nothing practical to show our appreciation of it? Or would it not be, rather, an encumbrance of just material rites which, by losing their intention, would also lose their efficacy? For a Christian, nothing is more pressing than to know how to remember that God loves him, that God loves him to the extreme of death on the Cross. The Mass carries on this remembrance. "I will remember from memory," says St. Thomas in reference to the Mass, "and my soul swoons in me from love."

We should, therefore, assist at Mass with an

alert and attentive remembrance, that is to say, with great faith. Faith is an infused remembrance which is awakened, quickened and nourished by the memorial of Jesus. Let us grow mature in faith; and as one practical help in doing this, let us dedicate our Christian remembrance to the Blessed Virgin and to the Saints. They will make our memorial of the Lord's death shine resplendently. Indeed, the Mass is that point of unspeakable contemporaneity in which time is linked to eternity in a wonderful osmosis of love —love from which we can draw on the merits of Jesus and of the Saints. The spiritual maternity of Mary, the paternity of St. Dominic, the immense fraternal Christian charity of all the Saints are concentrated in the heart of Jesus and pour over us with redemptive Blood, through the wounds which will eternally bear witness to the great price of our redemption.

It is very important for us to appreciate in the concrete and practical order that in the entire world there is just *one* sacrifice sanctioned by God, namely the crucifixion of Jesus Christ. It is the only one that really perdures, not only in the tangible rights of the liturgy, but in a mystical manner, in the perennial life and in the precious death of the faithful who die in the state of grace. St. Gregory the Great admonishes us that "when we celebrate the mysteries of the Passion, we must imitate what we do. For Jesus is not truly and efficaciously a sacrificial victim for us before His Father, except when we make sacrificial victims of ourselves by entering into the dispositions of His divine nature." This is why at Mass we must not only recall Jesus' sacrifice, but also the co-redemptive work of the Virgin, and the immolated life and death of the Saints. It is the ideal moment for us to be introduced into the community of the saints, despite our unworthiness—a community such as Fra Angelico has portrayed it, all of us gathered together at the foot of the Cross, drawn there by prayer and sacred desire.

Imagine how the holy Virgin knew how to

administer her treasure and how she safeguarded the body and blood of Jesus which have saved us: she never ceased to offer them in sacrifice to God. May she also gather us and preserve us in her maternal heart in order to offer us to God in remembrance of the Passion of Jesus, in living witness of it.

The priesthood and the Mass were the inexhaustable sources from which the saints drew their energies of devotion—the great compassion for instance which marked the life of St. Dominic. No one can teach us better than he how to assist at Mass. And if we are priests, no one better than he can teach us how to celebrate it and to live it in all ways. Like St. Dominic, with our arms in the form of a cross, let us crucify the whole of our being in sacrifice to God. Let us behold with faith and love the Host and Chalice which the priest offers to the adoration of the faithful. Let us intimately unite our soul and body with Jesus crucified, by offering ourselves entirely to Him through the hands of the priest. Let us put our entire life and our death on the paten and in the chalice.

"The Mass is the work of the loftiest contemplation," says St. Vincent Ferrer. And St. Peter of Verona, while consecrating the blood of the Lord, constantly dedicated his own blood to martyrdom.

Under the patronage of St. Mary Magdalene who witnessed the flowing of the redemptive blood, by the invocation to Our Lady of the Precious Blood, let all of us Christians learn the spirit of our vocation which is the *quotidie morior*, a daily death for Christ, the permanent sacrifice of ourselves by union with the Eucharistic Sacrifice of Jesus. We have no other means in the world that are better proportioned to our salvation: it is in fact our own salvation through the Cross. At each Mass in which we participate —and in spirit we can participate constantly in this continuous celebration—nothing less is demanded of us than the sacrifice of our life: first of all the immediate portions of our existence which are the week, the day, the hour and which we must project entirely into God in an effort which solemnly engages our whole soul.

Nothing is as absolutely necessary as to love Jesus Christ—totally, immediately, practically, in terms that carry us across the borders of our selfishness to the limitless horizon of His Divine Person—and nothing should ever prevent us from proving this love to Him through the constant oblation of ourselves in remembrance of His sacrifice. Tribulations, anguish, death itself (as St. Paul said) should only make us penetrate further into His blessed Passion, to discover there the vastness of God's love and the mysterious depths of tenderness and understanding present in the Heart of Christ, our King.

If you enjoyed this book, you may be interested in other volumes included in "The Carmel Series on Christian Life." For free catalogs and information, write the publisher: